U.S. Department of Justice
Office of Justice Programs
National Institute of Justice

I0449232

National Institute of Justice

Research Report

The Role of Police Psychology in Controlling Excessive Force

About the National Institute of Justice

The National Institute of Justice, a component of the Office of Justice Programs, is the research and development agency of the U.S. Department of Justice. NIJ was established to prevent and reduce crime and to improve the criminal justice system. Specific mandates established by Congress in the Omnibus Crime Control and Safe Streets Act of 1968, as amended, and the Anti-Drug Abuse Act of 1988 direct the National Institute of Justice to:

- *Sponsor special projects and research and development programs* that will improve and strengthen the criminal justice system and reduce or prevent crime.

- *Conduct national demonstration projects* that employ innovative or promising approaches for improving criminal justice.

- *Develop new technologies* to fight crime and improve criminal justice.

- *Evaluate the effectiveness of criminal justice programs* and identify programs that promise to be successful if continued or repeated.

- *Recommend actions* that can be taken by Federal, State, and local governments as well as private organizations to improve criminal justice.

- *Carry out research on criminal behavior.*

- *Develop new methods of crime prevention* and reduction of crime and delinquency.

The National Institute of Justice has a long history of accomplishments, including the following:

- Basic research on career criminals that led to the development of special police and prosecutor units to deal with repeat offenders.

- Research that confirmed the link between drugs and crime.

- The research and development program that resulted in the creation of police body armor that has meant the difference between life and death to hundreds of police officers.

- Pioneering scientific advances such as the research and development of DNA analysis to positively identify suspects and eliminate the innocent from suspicion.

- The evaluation of innovative justice programs to determine what works, including drug enforcement, community policing, community anti-drug initiatives, prosecution of complex drug cases, drug testing throughout the criminal justice system, and user accountability programs.

- Creation of a corrections information-sharing system that enables State and local officials to exchange more efficient and cost-effective concepts and techniques for planning, financing, and constructing new prisons and jails.

- Operation of the world's largest criminal justice information clearinghouse, a resource used by State and local officials across the Nation and by criminal justice agencies in foreign countries.

The Institute Director, who is appointed by the President and confirmed by the Senate, establishes the Institute's objectives, guided by the priorities of the Office of Justice Programs, the Department of Justice, and the needs of the criminal justice field. The Institute actively solicits the views of criminal justice professionals to identify their most critical problems. Dedicated to the priorities of Federal, State, and local criminal justice agencies, research and development at the National Institute of Justice continues to search for answers to what works and why in the Nation's war on drugs and crime.

The Role of Police Psychology in Controlling Excessive Force

Ellen M. Scrivner, Ph.D.

A Report Presented to the National Institute of Justice

April 1994

U.S. Department of Justice
Office of Justice Programs

National Institute of Justice

Craig Uchida
Acting Director
Office of Criminal Justice Research

Ellen M. Scrivner, Ph.D.
Visiting Fellow
National Institute of Justice

This project was supported under award number 92–IJ–CX–0002 from the National Institute of Justice, Office of Justice Programs, U.S. Department of Justice. The report was prepared by Ellen M. Scrivner, Ph.D., Visiting Fellow, National Institute of Justice. Opinions or points of view expressed in this document are those of the author and do not necessarily reflect the official position or policies of the U.S. Department of Justice.

NCJ 146206

Summary

This report discusses the role of police psychologists in preventing and identifying individual police officers at risk for use of excessive, nonlethal force and the factors that contribute to police use of excessive force in performing their duties.

A sample of 65 police psychologists were asked what types of professional services they provided to police departments and how these services were used to control the use of force. They were also asked to characterize officers who abuse force and to suggest intervention strategies based on police psychology that could help police managers reduce the incidence of excessive force.

Results of the survey indicated that psychologists were more involved with counseling and evaluating functions than with training and monitoring of police officer behavior, and counseling was more likely to take place as a response to excessive-force incidents than as a means of prevention.

Five different profiles of officers with excessive-force problems emerged:

■ Officers with personality disorders such as lack of empathy for others, and antisocial, narcissistic, and abusive tendencies.

■ Officers with previous job-related experiences, such as involvement in justifiable police shootings.

■ Officers who experienced early career stage problems having to do with their impressionability, impulsiveness, low tolerance for frustration, and general need for strong supervision.

■ Officers who had a dominant, heavy-handed patrol style that is particularly sensitive to challenge and provocation.

■ Officers who had personal problems such as separation, divorce, or perceived loss of status that caused extreme anxiety and destabilized job functioning.

Police psychologists used psychological tests and clinical interviews to evaluate police candidates to the near exclusion of other screening methods. Lack of coordination of core psychologist functions was seen to be a major impediment to the delivery of effective and credible psychological services in police departments. Psychologists favored increased monitoring and training as a means of reducing the use of excessive force.

Contents

Part 1. Introduction

In March 1991, the contentious debate on police use of force was reawakened. Repeated showings of the videotape that documented Rodney King's treatment by police officers created nationwide concern about police abuse of citizens. The Department of Justice called for research to determine the nature, extent, and best means of control of use of force by the Nation's police officers. To develop an information base for subsequent policy initiatives, the National Institute of Justice (NIJ) sponsored studies of key issues related to police use of force. One was a nationwide survey of police psychologists to learn more about the characteristics of officers who abuse force and what psychologists recommend to control police violence. Key conclusions show:

■ Reasons for excessive force are complex. Individual officer characteristics are one element, but organizational practices are also implicated.

■ Excessive force can be reduced by strengthening supervisory oversight and providing training that builds resistance to provocational patrol situations.

■ Comprehensive prevention strategies are preferable to a crisis response for managing excessive force and are a better use of scarce resources.

Law enforcement agencies have long been concerned about excessive force and its costly price tag. Their concerns heighten during times of community turbulence when police chiefs are faced with balancing internal pressures and external demands to control police conduct. This study suggests that police managers looking for ways to control the use of excessive force need to understand the psychological dynamics in play in such situations. To this end, they can tap the resources they already have—the psychologists who work with their departments.

The research discussed in this report explored how police departments use the psychologists they hire. Departments hire psychologists for their expertise in understanding human behavior, including aggression and violent behavior, and in understanding what contributes to behavioral change. At the outset of this study, however, it was unknown if police departments were making full use of these skills and using psychologists as a resource for proactive problem solving, since there had been no previous systematic attempt to find out this information. If police departments use psychologists only for clinical crises, they are adopting a strategy analogous to incident-driven policing. They unnecessarily narrow the scope of psychological interventions available to help them.

Launching a Systemwide Response

One example of how psychologists can intervene in an excessive-force problem occurred in a large East Coast police department. When changing demographics brought a prevailing excessive force problem to the forefront, this department responded by developing comprehensive, systemic strategies to reduce excessive force and used its psychological services division as one resource in this effort. The department encouraged its psychological services and training divisions to collaborate in reaching these objectives:

■ Change the traditional, individual counseling model to one addressing excessive-force incidents from the perspective of officer-situation-offender interactions. This made it possible to collect data that developed a fuller understanding of how complex interactions present "at risk" conditions for excessive force.

■ Provide the new information to the training division. The new insights highlighting the complex of personal, situational, and offender interactions enabled trainers to incorporate realistic patrol situations into their programs.

■ Present these data to all field training officer classes and to first line supervisor schools. This sensitized participants to the criticality of their roles in changing excessive force behavior.

■ Present research findings on officer-situation-offender interactions to command policymakers. This enabled them to make more informed policy reviews on the use of excessive force (Scrivner, 1988).

This example illustrates how a psychological intervention became one component of a proactive organizational response to the problem. In contrast to using the psychologist only to counsel individual officers, this strategy used the counseling, training, and research functions of the psychologist to provide the department with comprehensive behavioral data on the psychological determinants of excessive force. The information was structured to preserve the confidentiality of privileged communications and was used constructively for training and policymaking. Essentially, this strategy established new organizational feedback loops throughout the department, with the psychology/training/management loop as only one example. When combined with changes recommended by an appointed commission, including the implementation of community policing, the strategies enabled the department to improve its management of excessive force.

One of the goals of the research described in this report was to determine if this example was relatively rare or reflected how police departments generally use psychologists to help them deal with excessive-force problems.

Research Questions

To develop information on the status of police psychological services, police psychologists were interviewed about their current practices and how these addressed excessive force. They were asked:

■ What types of professional services do you provide in police departments?

■ How are these services used by police departments to control the use of force?

■ How do you characterize officers who abuse force? Are they "bad apples," rogue cops, products of organizational failure, or all of these? Are their acts a unique type of violence in the workplace?

■ Are there promising intervention strategies based on police psychology that can help police managers reduce the incidence of excessive force?

Their answers to these questions form the basis for this report. A brief overview of the history of police psychology is presented first to help readers understand why police departments hire psychologists and what they are hired to do.

Part 2. History of Psychological Services to Police

Psychologists began to work with police agencies in the late 1960's, (Reiser, 1972; Reese, 1987). Recommendations from the 1968 National Advisory Commission on Civil Disorder Report, which followed the urban riots of that year, called for screening methods that would improve the quality of the police officers hired. These recommendations, and the availability of discretionary funds through the Law Enforcement Assistance Administration, encouraged police departments to seek the expertise of psychologists to help them select emotionally stable candidates with personal characteristics suitable for police work. Thus, one of the first police psychology functions involved preemployment screening of applicants using psychological tests and assessments, a fairly traditional responsibility for psychologists but one that was new to the police personnel function.

Later, clinical services were requested and, by 1980, both applicant screening and counseling to help officers cope with the stressful nature of policing were identified as primary activities of police psychologists (Stratton, 1980).

Reese (1987) detailed the evolution of police psychology and defined psychological services as the professional services of credentialed mental health professionals, such as psychiatrists, psychologists, and psychiatric social workers, who work on a regular basis with police departments and who provide a wide array of services. While many of the services were specific to mental health, Reese also showed how psychologists brought new sets of intervention skills to police agencies in areas such as a critical incident response for police shootings, hostage-barricade negotiation skills, criminal profiling, and forensic hypnosis.

The initiation of stress management training in police departments paralleled the developments cited by Reese. A 1984 FBI report on State and local police training needs identified the predominant training need to be assistance in handling personal stress. This study led psychologists to develop a variety of programs to address stressors unique to law enforcement. Currently, these programs are framed as "wellness training" and are consistent with a trend to stress mental health prevention strategies.

The role of police psychology further expanded over the last decade despite the findings of a 1979 survey of police departments that did not look promising for police psychology. In that survey 62 percent of the 112 respondents indicated no intentions to expand or start psychological services in the forthcoming two years; only 18 percent anticipated future use of psychologists (Parisher, Rios, and Riley, 1979).

A 1988 survey by Delprine and Bahn, however, showed a substantial change. This survey of 336 municipal and State police agencies found that half of the 232 respondents used the services of psychologists and also endorsed the need to expand this practice. Psychological screening of police recruits, counseling of police officers for job-related stress and personal and family problems were primary activities identified in the survey. Other activities included a range of differentially applied training activities such as training in human relations. All have implications for managing excessive force.

Systematic survey findings were consistent with a growing recognition of police psychology as a distinct field in professional psychology. Key events in the 1980's formalized this distinction and included two major conferences on police psychology sponsored by the FBI Academy; recognition of police psychology by the American Psychological Association (APA) through the formation of a police psychology section in its division of psychologists in public service; and the formation of a police psychology section within the International Association of Chiefs of Police (IACP).

These developments strengthened the professional dimensions of the field and encouraged growth of a police psychology literature. They led to participation in program symposia and workshops at the APA and IACP annual conventions and to the development of policy guidelines for specific practices. There was more professional commentary on public policy issues relative to policing, including APA testimony before congressional hearings.

A more comprehensive and multifaceted role was established for an active police psychology presence in the Nation's police departments.

Current research findings corroborate the growth of psychological services to police. Although preemployment screening and counseling still command a major share of police psychologists' attention, several departments have institutionalized a broader role for psychologists, one that defines the police psychologist as an organizational resource for consultation on policy and planning related to effective use of the organization's human resources (Kirschman, Scrivner, Ellison, and Marcy, 1992; Scrivner, 1992).

Confidentiality and Other Credibility Issues

Despite this substantial growth, questions have been raised about the credibility of police psychological services, primarily with respect to confidentiality and other aspects of professional practice. Those who challenge the viability of confidential services may not be aware of the importance of following APA ethical standards and adhering to State laws that govern psychological practice and licensure. Maintaining confidentiality is both a professional and practical concern because of risks to licensure and threats of malpractice. In paramilitary organizations such risks are not always clearly understood, but in all likelihood most officers and administrators would agree that any breach of confidentiality would destroy these services.

Other issues related to credibility include maintaining clear distinctions as to who is the client—the individual officer or the organization—and avoiding the serious conflicts implicit in dual-role relationships; and ensuring use of reliable and valid methodologies (particularly for preemployment screening) that adhere to guidelines of the Equal Employment Opportunity Commission and conform to the Americans With Disabilities Act and civil rights legislation. These pressing demands have dominated psychologists' attention and are central to the integrity of the field. Strategies to respond to excessive force have received less attention.

The Research

For the first two decades that police departments employed psychologists, lethal force was of greater concern than nonlethal force. Shootings by police were traumatic incidents that created strong emotional reactions from the officers who did the shooting. The need to provide psychological support for officers involved in them was clear. Studies showed that departments gradually saw the need to provide psychological support services immediately following these incidents.

That same level of concern did not generally carry over to the inappropriate use of nonlethal force. Officers might be given evaluations for their fitness for duty, but psychological support services were not widely available. Over the past few years, however, greater attention has been given both by police departments and by researchers as to why some officers use excessive force.

Studies have looked at the various factors that contribute to the use of excessive force. Some have explored the use of skill-based training to help officers avoid potentially violent situations and concluded that violent incidents do not erupt in a split second but may result from the coming together of many elements. It is becoming clearer that background events in the officer's life, the culture of policing itself, variable police policies on the use of force, and community conditions may all be determinants of excessive force.

Multiple determinants of excessive force speak to a need for police departments to develop systematic safeguards to reduce abuse of force instead of relying on preemployment screening alone to predict abusive behavior. Two reports that followed the Rodney King beating, the 1991 report of the Independent Commission To Study the Los Angeles Police Department (known as the Christopher Commission) and the 1992 Los Angeles County Sheriff's report by James G. Kolt and staff, questioned the effectiveness of current psychological screening to predict propensity for violence. These reports supported the concept of assessment but raised concerns about the scope and methods of current psychological screening. The Christopher Commission further recommended greater scrutiny of a candidate's past behavior beyond the drug use and sexual behavior emphases in police background investigations.

Research studies now under way are exploring ways to improve the accuracy of predictions of violent behavior. They may hold promise to strengthen police screening. An overview of these and the literature pertaining to nonlethal force is presented in the appendix to this report.

Conclusions From the Literature

The literature on nonlethal force is growing, indicating wide interest in this area, but a full understanding of the scope of viable interventions remains limited. A single abusive incident can ignite latent community hostilities, threaten the police chief's job, and still leave police officers unclear about how they could have acted differently. Having met with some success in curtailing the use of lethal force, police policymakers face the equally difficult problem of reducing physically violent police-citizen confrontations at a time when the Nation's communities are experiencing increased violence. A number of factors have been cited to account for police use of excessive force, such as racial and ethnic tensions, the fire power of urban criminals, and the number of drug-addicted offenders.

The methods of police psychology offer an added resource for police organizations in their efforts to reduce excessive force. The scope of these methods, however, needs to be clarified and the core police psychology functions examined for their effectiveness in controlling police abuse of force.

The research described in this report examined one element of the excessive force problem, the police psychology practices and interventions applied to reduce excessive force. The examination was undertaken from the perspective of individual officer behavior and from the organizational practices that shape police behavior. It is anticipated that the information provided in this study will help police managers control unjustified use of force more effectively.

Part 3. Research Methodology

This study interviewed police psychologists representing 50 of the largest police departments in cities with populations that exceed 100,000. Two sources were used to identify the cities: *Uniform Crime Reports for the United States* (1990) and the *Jeffers Directory* (1990). Police personnel divisions for these cities were contacted for names and addresses of the police psychologists who provided services to their departments. In most instances, the departments provided the name of more than one psychologist.

A total of 95 psychologists who worked with police in the 50 cities were identified. The 95 psychologist subjects were sent a letter requesting their participation and explaining the scope and methods of the study. They were provided with written guarantees of confidentiality and assured that their departments would not be identified. The privacy of these data and of research participants is protected under Federal law [section 524(a) of the Crime Control and Safe Streets Act (28 CFR Part 11)].

Nine of the psychologists were excluded from the study because their contact with the police department was too limited. Only 6 (6 percent) refused to participate. However, 15 psychologists (15.8 percent) who agreed to participate were unable to be scheduled for interviews because of conflicts due to vacations, time zone differences, schedule demands, or possibly a lack of interest. Hence, 65 psychologists (68 percent of those contacted) participated in the study.

Data were collected using a telephone interview protocol that included 61 questions covering the major police psychology functions central to excessive force as well as participant background information and general opinions.

Interview drafts were pretested with police psychologists who met monthly in a consortium (Law Enforcement Behavioral Science Association). The psychologists were not participants in the study but served as a focus group convened at different times throughout the research to explore the dimensions of the study findings.

Operational Definition of Excessive Force

At the outset of the study, the researchers found that police departments did not apply a uniform definition of excessive force. (Another NIJ study, in process, will provide a national determination of how police policies define excessive force.)

In this study, excessive force was defined as a violation of a police department's use-of-force policy by an incumbent officer that was serious enough to warrant a referral to the police psychologist. The operational definition presents certain constraints because it limits selected interview responses to only the most serious offenders. Data were not captured on officers who use excessive force but are not referred to the department psychologist or on officers who use force but against whom charges are not pressed. The officers studied are clearly a population that warrants empirical investigation in order to learn about the determinants of excessive force. However, the limitations need to be kept in mind by readers of this report.

A further constraint is related to the methodology of telephone interviews which, in this case, did not allow for psychologists to check the accuracy of their responses against official records.

The Sample

The 65 police psychologists interviewed in the study, and the departments they served, had the following characteristics:

■ They had spent an average of 12.5 years as police psychologists, 9.8 of them with their current department.

■ The median size of police departments they worked in had a sworn strength of 1,264.

■ 32 percent of the psychologists provided services to a single department; 68 percent served more than one department.

■ The median number of departments served by a single psychologist was 10.

■ 35 percent of the psychologists held salaried positions within the department.

■ 25 percent held a command staff position.

■ 65 percent served as external consultants.

Participants in the study were interviewed about their work in 50 departments, but as a group they actually provided services to a total of 913 police departments. For the most part, the other departments had limited sworn strength and served less populated jurisdictions than the 50 departments in the sample.

These data indicate that the police psychologists interviewed were highly experienced and had worked a long time both as salaried employees and as consultants. The finding that 25 percent of the sample were on police command staffs is a further measure of the continued growth in status of police psychological services in police organizations.

Part 4. Analysis of Major Findings

As noted, the psychologists were asked about the core functions of police psychologists that had relevance to officer use of excessive force. These are evaluation (preemployment screening and fitness for duty), monitoring of police behavior, training initiatives, and counseling programs.

Their responses to these questions are presented in this section. Each major finding is accompanied by supporting data and discussion of its significance.

Core Functions of Police Psychologists

Psychologists were more involved with counseling, evaluating, and training than with monitoring the behavior of police officers.

- 77 percent provided counseling services.

- 71 percent conducted preemployment screening.

- 54 percent conducted training classes.

- 52 percent conducted evaluations of fitness for duty.

- 42 percent monitored officer behavior.

Psychologists counseled, screened, and trained police officers more frequently than they performed other functions. Over half of the sample (54 percent) provided all three of these services but not necessarily to the same departments; 29 percent restricted their activities to providing counseling, and 17 percent did only evaluation work including preemployment screening and fitness evaluations.

More psychologists conducted training for recruits (52 percent) and inservice training (54 percent) than for other groups such as first line supervisors (46 percent), command staff (40 percent), and field training officers (35 percent). This training covered a span of topics ranging from hostage negotiations to handling the mentally ill, but stress management training (51 percent) was provided with the greatest frequency.

Fifty-two percent of the psychologists conducted evaluations of fitness for duty. An additional 23 percent referred officers they were counseling to other psychologists for these evaluations to avoid the conflict of interest of treating and evaluating the same individual. Only 25 percent of the 65 psychologists had no involvement with fitness evaluations. Estimates of the average number of fitness evaluations and referrals that resulted from excessive-force incidents ranged from 15 to 20 percent; other fitness referrals were based on officers exhibiting aberrant job behavior, substance abuse, suicide potential, and clinical depression.

The service least frequently provided was the monitoring function. Forty-two percent of the psychologists used systematic oversight methods to track officer performance for purposes of validating preemployment screening and for assessing the success of training and counseling. Only 23 percent used it for early identification of police officers who are developing excessive-force problems.

The monitoring function. The monitoring function links prevention and remedial interventions by identifying and responding to behavior cues that signify potential performance problems. The monitoring function permits early intervention in police problems before they get out of control.

Psychologists reported that a majority of the police departments represented in the sample used some form of monitoring, but 58 percent did not include the psychologist in these efforts. Computer tracking of complaints appeared to be the most prevalent form of early warning used.

While computer tracking may provide useful management information, its utility is questionable for changing behavior because the behavior is relatively well developed by the time it is flagged by the computer. It is flagged after the fact rather than as a "warning," so excessive force behavior may already be entrenched, making change more difficult. Change can be further constrained by the acrimony that develops from lengthy investigations of complaints. The squad may support the officer, believing he or she is being railroaded for doing his or her job. Hence, earlier interventions that are responsive to qualitative and not just quantitative events, and that are consistent with principles of changing behavior, need to be considered.

There are several nonintrusive ways to monitor behavior. The method most preferred by psychologists is a variant of an early warning system that involves supervisors as a key element in reducing excessive force. This method systematically tracks a range of "marker" behaviors that signify a need for supervisory intervention when they begin to occur consistently. The observations of the supervisor are combined with the expertise of the psychologist to understand the significance of an officer's behavior changes. Then appropriate interventions and followup are initiated before the markers evolve into excessive force problems.

The following are some examples of marker behavior:

■ Squad concerns develop about an officer getting someone hurt.

■ An officer acquires nicknames signifying forceful arrests.

■ An officer's prisoners accumulate injuries.

■ An officer's insubordinate behavior begins to increase.

Such markers, and others, come to a supervisor's attention without peers revealing them and before formal complaints are filed. They are the type of information that circulates throughout a precinct, and as they begin to accumulate, they warn supervisors of the need to take action.

In this model, psychologists train supervisors to detect precursors of problem behavior and how to act upon them through intervention support before the accrual of official complaints. Supervisors are trained to give ongoing attention to a wide range of behavior in order to structure an appropriate intervention and, when necessary, can use the psychologist in an advisory capacity. The intervention may take varied forms but is essentially designed to respond to a particular officer's needs and at a

level when behavior change is generally easier to accomplish. In contrast to paper work drills or a bureaucratic response, this method is a function of good supervision with a human resource focus. It assists supervisors to be better managers and more responsive to the needs of subordinates.

Monitoring police behavior serves other purposes beyond early identification and intervention. It is not only a vehicle for training but also provides for a more sustained level of posttraining contact than can be achieved with 1-day training sessions on excessive force. It conforms to recommendations by Reiss (1980) to involve supervisors as a key element in violence reduction, and it also develops significant information to enable police managers to evaluate the influence of policy and procedures on police behavior. Finally, it examines individual officer behavior within the context of organizational influences that affect use of excessive force.

The strong evidence showing administrative emphasis on referrals for counseling and fitness evaluations provides further support for increasing the monitoring function. The fitness evaluation, in particular, generally occurs after the problem has gone on for some time and is frequently a prelude to separation from the agency. There may be some cases where this practice is the only alternative. For many officers, however, earlier psychological interventions may preclude fitness evaluations.

Finally, the need for earlier interventions parallels the "broken windows" arguments (Wilson and Kelling, 1982) that had a significant impact on how police leadership came to reframe the crime control mission. The argument that early signs of community deterioration were forerunners of more serious criminal problems could be applied to the human behavior dimension of the police organization. Police managers would be well-advised to pay attention to the clear signals that suggest deterioration in officer behavior, the behavioral equivalent of "broken windows," *before* it results in excessive force complaints. If police treat abuse of force as they do serious crime in the community, by waiting until it happens, then their personnel practices, like incident-driven policing, constitute a reactive rather than proactive response. An incident-driven frame of reference can create institutional barriers to effective intervention and can also have implications for how well the services of psychologists are integrated into a police agency.

Integration of Core Functions

Lack of coordination of core psychologist functions was a major impediment to the delivery of effective and credible psychological services in police departments.

The 65 psychologists were asked to cite impediments to their delivery of psychological services.

■ 77 percent of psychologists cited lack of coordination with the department.

■ 72 percent cited program credibility.

■ 65 percent said psychological services did not receive priority.

■ 57 percent cited clinical crisis orientation.

■ 51 percent cited dependence on individual rather than organizational interventions.

The data create concerns that poor integration of psychological services, as evidenced by lack of coordination, represents a major impediment to provision of effective psychological services in police departments. Moreover, many departments seemed to have adopted a crisis model with a case-by-case, individual, clinical focus to using police psychologists; they seemed to be using them on an "as needed" basis rather than for systematic human resource development. These data have particular relevance for psychological interventions specific to excessive force because a poorly coordinated crisis response that does not monitor or follow up on behavior change may be comparable to putting a bandaid on a gaping wound. It is not clear from these data whether poorly coordinated services also affect program credibility or if this finding implicates the actual practices of psychologists.

Core Functions and Excessive Force

Counseling interventions were used to respond to excessive force more frequently than were other psychologists' functions including those that focus on prevention.

Psychologists were asked about their interventions with respect to use of excessive force.

■ 79 percent counseled officers charged with excessive force.

■ 51 percent covered excessive force in stress management training.

■ 25 percent conducted training specific to excessive force.

■ 23 percent monitored behavior for signs of excessive force.

These findings are consistent with those previously cited about how police departments use psychologists. Of particular significance is the limited amount of training that was specifically directed to excessive force and the low level of monitoring. Both provide further evidence that the array of available psychological services have not been integrated systematically in police departments. These findings lead to other questions on whether police psychology needs to devote more attention to how law enforcement practices are changing and how innovations from psychology can be used to respond to contemporary police challenges.

Innovations in Excessive Force Training

Only 16 of the psychologists interviewed (25 percent) responded to the excessive-force challenge by developing training models based on psychological theories and research related to human functioning under adverse conditions and in highly charged situations. The training described by this group represents innovative and promising trends. Programs addressed:

■ Cultural sensitivity and diversity.

■ Intervention by fellow officers to stop the use of excessive force.

■ Perceptual processes and threat assessment.

■ Decisionmaking under highly charged conditions.

■ Psychological methods of situation control.

■ Patrol de-escalation and defusing techniques that teach a tactical response but also respond to the fear stimulated by confrontations.

■ Anger management programs that use self-assessment and self-management techniques for providing individual feedback to officers on how variable levels of anger influence judgment.

■ Training in verbal control and communication, including "verbal judo" and conflict resolution.

These training models are based on principles of adult learning. They require class participation and interaction and use patrol simulations, role playing, peer interaction with feedback, and videotaping of simulated interactions. They emphasize a new dimension in law enforcement training and focus on nonphysical skill development but not at the expense of officer survival. Moreover, they are compatible with a community policing philosophy.

Stress Management Training and Excessive Force

Of particular interest is the finding that 51 percent of psychologists addressed excessive force only in stress management training. Clearly, stress management training is important, and it would be difficult to argue that use of force confrontations are not stressful. However, framing excessive force as a stress issue raises several questions:

■ Can that notion be supported by research?

■ Does treating it this way encourage the perception that stress is an excuse for excessive force?

■ Does it reinforce an adversarial relationship between police and citizens?

The fact that stress management training in police departments has not been evaluated systematically poses an additional concern. Beyond anecdotal evidence, the paucity of empirical evidence on how stress affects general police performance suggests shaky ground for addressing stress in relationship to excessive force. A more viable training focus would incorporate clear policy statements that clarify the tolerance limits for use of force and conceptualize excessive force as a patrol risk that needs to be managed by applying a range of specialized skills. This represents a proactive stance that is generally considered to be more effective for changing behavior.

Other training and excessive-force findings showed that many psychologists who conducted training in police departments discussed excessive force in training but not within the context of a specific block of instruction. Of the groups that psychologists trained, first line supervisors received less instruction on excessive force (32 percent) than recruits (46 percent); field training officers received even less (23 percent). Yet psychologists said first line supervisors had greater influence on officers prone to excessive force than other police personnel significant to an officer's career. This finding suggests that police departments may need to consider shifting the emphasis in supervisor training from a paperwork focus to one that incorporates larger behavioral issues in order to improve the management of excessive force. This level of supervisory training could also incorporate instruction on implementing early warning behavioral monitoring.

Clinical Descriptions of Excessive Force and Systemic Interventions

Five different profiles were identified when psychologists characterized officers at risk for excessive force. The popular stereotype that a "few bad apples" are responsible for most, if not all, excessive force complaints was not supported by these responses; both individual personality characteristics and organizational influences were identified as contributing to abuse of force.

The following responses emerged when psychologists were asked about the characteristics of police officers referred to them for counseling because of excessive-force problems:

■ 16 percent had personality disorders that placed them at chronic risk for excessive use of force.

■ 17 percent had previous job-related experiences that could place them at risk for abuse of force.

■ 18 percent were young and immature officers at early stages in their police careers.

■ 21 percent developed patrol styles that incorporated the routine use of force.

■ 28 percent experienced personal problems.

These responses suggest that personality characteristics are only one element of excessive force and that risk for this behavior is intensified by other experiences, some of which implicate organizational practices. The characterizations do not support the notion that personality or individual pathology is solely responsible for excessive force, a notion that would provide a more simplistic basis for understanding and responding to behavior. Rather, these data address a number of factors that are systemic and contribute to excessive force in police departments.

In distinguishing the features of these five profiles, only one resembled the "bad apple" characterization: the chronic risks for excessive force, the smallest group of at-risk officers.

Chronic risk. This group was distinguished from other at-risk groups because the persistence of involvement suggests serious personality disorders. These officers were described as having pervasive and enduring personality traits (in contrast to acquired characteristics) that are manifested in antisocial, narcissistic, paranoid, or abusive tendencies. These conditions interfere with judgment and interactions with others, particularly when officers perceive challenges or threats to their authority. Such officers generally lack empathy for others. They tend to be exploitative and manipulative and may also be involved in substance abuse. These characteristics tend to persist

through life but may be intensified by the nature of police work. They may not be fully apparent at preemployment screening.

Individuals with these personality patterns generally do not learn from experience or accept responsibility for their own behavior, so they are at greater risk for repeated complaints. Thus, they may appear as the sole source of problems in police departments. However, the other identified profiles show that groups of officers with different characteristics were actually seen by psychologists more frequently. It may be that the chronic risk group were seen less frequently by psychologists because they had already been recommended for termination through disciplinary procedures in response to repeated complaints. Another explanation may be that fewer of the chronic-risk group were hired.

Job-related experience. Officers with prior histories of involvement in job-related traumatic situations, such as justifiable police shootings, represented a second group of officers who were profiled as being at risk for excessive force, but for totally different reasons from the first group. These officers were not unsocialized, egocentric, or violent. In fact, personality factors appeared to have less to do with their vulnerability to excessive force than the emotional baggage they had accumulated from involvement in prior incidents. Frequently, these officers had become isolated from their squads and were verging on burnout or had symptoms of Post Traumatic Stress Disorder. Because of their need to keep symptoms hidden, it was some time before they came to anyone's attention. When they did, it was often because of an excessive force situation in which they "lost it."

In contrast to the chronic at-risk group, officers in this group are amenable to critical-incident treatment interventions, but to be fully effective, these need to be applied soon after their involvement in the traumatic incident. There is a wealth of literature now available that details recommended department policies and procedures to manage these incidents. The studies recommend training and psychological debriefings with followup to minimize the development of psychological symptoms. Researchers have speculated that job-related traumatic incidents, when untreated, could result in excessive force. The findings presented in this report verify the anecdotal evidence and show that some officers who accumulate prior traumatic incidents could develop problems with excessive force.

Early career stage problems. The third group profiled by the sample were described as young and inexperienced officers, frequently seen as "hotdogs," "badge happy," "macho," or generally immature. Totally enthused about their jobs but not fully developed as police officers, these officers may cross the line on excessive force before they know it.

In contrast to other inexperienced officers, this group was characterized as highly impressionable and impulsive, with low tolerance for frustration. Despite the greater frequency with which they are seen by psychologists, they bring positive attributes to their work; peers and supervisors can be persuaded that they will "outgrow" these tendencies and learn with experience. Unfortunately, the positive qualities can deteriorate early in their careers if they have not been appropriately focused through strong field training officer experience or through other corrective experiences.

These officers were described as needing strong supervision and highly structured field training. To assign them to a field training officer with limited street experience, a common practice, only magnifies the problem. Because they are strongly influenced by the police culture, such new recruits are more apt to change their behavior if their mentors are experienced and respected officers who demonstrate a professional demeanor in their dealings with citizens.

This finding has decided implications for field training officer programs. Instruction on excessive force for field training officers is critical as is the need for well-developed selection criteria for field training officers and appropriate matching of recruits and trainers. However, even with the best of programs some officers will not have the benefit

of these experiences and may require other interventions such as a change in their patrol environment. For this group, training, mentoring, and supervisory interventions may be more productive than relying only on individual counseling.

Patrol style. One could ask if immature new officers whose macho tendencies are left unattended become the more seasoned officers who use force as a matter of routine. Individuals who fit this profile were described as combining a dominant command presence with a heavy-handed patrol style that was particularly sensitive to challenge and provocation. Among these officers the use of force to show that they were in charge became the norm as their beliefs about how police work is done became more rigid.

Their behavior differs from that of members in the chronic risk group in that the behavior is acquired and can be changed with varying degrees of success. The longer the patterns continue, however, the more difficult change becomes. The officers become invested in police power, control, and authority and either lose interest or see little reason to change. Officers in this group are often labeled as "dinosaurs" in a changing police world marked by greater accountability to citizens.

These officers required strong supervision and training experiences early in their careers, and when they didn't get it their propensity to rely on force was reinforced. If at some point in their careers they were also detailed to a special unit with minimal supervision, this style may have been further reinforced. In many respects, members of this group may perceive their behavior as having been sanctioned by the organization. For intervention purposes, this group would be more responsive to peer program interventions or models like situational counseling in contrast to traditional individual counseling. Making them part of the solution, rather than part of the problem, may be central to changing their behavior.

Personal problems. The final and most frequently endorsed risk profile was made up of officers who experienced personal problems that destabilized their job functioning. Clearly, not all officers with personal problems engage in excessive force. Rather, this profile represented a particular type of officer whose level of personal adjustment becomes threatened by some personal loss such as separation, divorce, or even a perceived loss of status.

Psychologists questioned if officers who responded to loss this way may have elected police work for all the wrong reasons because, in contrast to police peers, they seemed to have a tenuous sense of self-worth and higher levels of anxiety that were well masked. These officers apparently functioned reasonably well until their personal situations changed to undermine their confidence and make it more difficult for them to deal with fear, animosity, and emotionally charged patrol situations.

Thus, patrol behavior can become erratic and show a host of signals, the precursors to problem behavior, before use of excessive force actually occurs. This group of officers, the most frequently seen for excessive-force problems, can be identified by supervisors who have been properly trained to observe and respond to precursors of problem behavior. Given their numbers, they encourage development of proactive monitoring to detect "marker behaviors" signifying that problems are brewing long before these problems are flagged by a computer because of several complaints. These officers do benefit from individual counseling, but earlier referrals would enhance the benefit and keep their personal situations from spilling over to their jobs.

These descriptive profiles suggest that there are different reasons for excessive force that call for different interventions. They indicate the complexity of the excessive force issue and the need for a system of interventions targeted to different groups of officers and at different phases of their careers. Members of some of the profiled groups are appropriate for individual counseling with psychologists while others may need organizational interventions. However, it is unlikely that all could be identified through the best of preemployment screening methods. Other

checks and balances need to be systematically incorporated if excessive force is to be effectively managed.

Preemployment Screening of Police Candidates

Psychologists used psychological tests and clinical interviews to evaluate police candidates to the near exclusion of other screening methods.

The data on preemployment screening practices are presented and discussed below. They show that not all the psychologists were engaged in screening; 46 of the 65 psychologists (71 percent) conducted screening. The tabled data are based on their responses. Psychologists used the following preemployment screening procedures:

- 96 percent used psychological tests.
- 91 percent used clinical interviews.
- 22 percent used risk assessment models.
- 15 percent used situational tests.
- 4 percent used job simulations.

Almost all the psychologists used a fairly traditional assessment procedure which has not incorporated innovation into psychological screening of police candidates. Arguably, job selection is an area where the need to build a stable normative base to validate the process may override innovation. However, the methods that are used less frequently may give better information about potential for excessive force. Unfortunately, they are also costly and time consuming to develop.

The screening practice used by most of the sample combined information from test results and the clinical interview, a generally recommended professional practice. A total of 78 percent indicated that the combined process was particularly important to evaluate propensity for violent behavior in job candidates.

Results of assessment instruments and interviews. The psychologists reported using a variety of assessment instruments that are primarily stan-

Common Testing Instruments

Minnesota Multiphasic Personality Inventory (MMPI—MMPI-2)

The MMPI is a 566-item questionnaire designed to identify major psychiatric disorders from responses to questions that form both clinical and validity test scales. Though developed in 1943 by Hathaway and McKinley, it has recently been revised in an updated form known as the MMPI-2 (567 items). The revision restandardized the normative sample and expanded the content to broaden settings where it can be used. Validation research with this test shows generally modest relationships between MMPI scale scores and police performance. Some of the scales, however, have been found to have strong relationships with aggression (Hargrave et al., 1986).

California Personality Inventory (CPI)

The CPI is a personality inventory derived from the MMPI but designed to assess "normal range" characteristics. Prediction equations have been developed that relate performance on certain scales to overall police effectiveness.

Sixteen Personality Factor/Clinical Analysis Questionnaire

These tests are presented together because the CAQ contains all items of the 16PF (Form A) in addition to specific clinical items. These tests were developed to provide objective measurement of primary behavioral dimensions and to provide measures of both normal and pathological behaviors.

Sentence Completion Test

This test is a brief projective test containing sentence stems that are filled out to express the individual's feelings and attitudes about the particular items.

Inwald Personality Inventory (IPI)

This personality inventory was developed specifically for law enforcement screening. It uses 26 behaviorally oriented scales to assess suitability for law enforcement. Profiles are compared to substantial normative police data, and the predictors are related to the criteria of absenteeism, lateness, and disciplinary interviews.

dardized measures of personality and cognitive functions but only a limited number of the tests are used consistently. They form the nucleus of a clinical test battery, and other tests are used to provide supplementary or supporting information.

■ 91 percent used the Minnesota Multiphasic Personality Inventory (MMPI–MMPI-2).

■ 54 percent used the California Personality Inventory (CPI).

■ 28 percent used the 16PF/Clinical Analysis Questionnaire.

■ 20 percent used sentence completion.

■ 15 percent used the Inwald Personality Inventory (IPI).

■ 15 percent used cognitive measures.

For the most part, these tests are paper-pencil inventories. With the exception of the varied cognitive measures, the identified tests generally assess personality characteristics. The cognitive tests measure particular abilities or aptitudes, such as reading or writing skills or general intelligence. Of the personality tests, the MMPI or MMPI-2, the revision of the original MMPI, is clearly the mainstay of the police selection process, followed by the CPI. This finding is consistent with other surveys on the tests most frequently used for police applicant screening (Ash, Slora, and Britton, 1990; Hargrave and Berner, 1984; Murphy, 1972). Brief descriptions of the most frequently used tests are presented in the box on this page.

Psychologists were asked to describe major indicators found in psychological test results that raised concerns about potential excessive force problems. They cited the following:

- Elevated MMPI scales,[1] cited by 72 percent.
- Personal rigidity, cited by 57 percent.
- Over-controlled hostility, cited by 28 percent.
- Impulsiveness, cited by 24 percent.
- Lack of socialization, cited by 15 percent.

They were also asked to describe major indicators that came to light during interviews. They cited the following:

- History of aggression, cited by 76 percent.
- Loss-of-control behavior, cited by 33 percent.
- History of abuse, cited by 33 percent.
- Disturbed relationships at work or school, cited by 33 percent.

Evaluating the results. Psychologists evaluate many factors in preemployment screening; the prevalent themes noted above address only a few of these factors. Rather, they provide a subset of personality dimensions that are relevant to the potential for abusing force. Since elevations on MMPI scales are related to some of the other indicators, distinctions across test indicators can appear blurred. Generally, the other tests are used with the MMPI either to evaluate certain characteristics or to corroborate MMPI results.

These data are more easily understood when considered within the context of specific personality dimensions, such as levels of impulsiveness, emotional control, hostility, and personal rigidity, as well as capacity for socialization. Assessment results that are well in excess of normal limits on these dimensions define what psychologists look for when they evaluate risk for excessive force. Psychologists use a variety of terms to characterize job candidates who are prone to aggressive, violent behavior, such as the following:

- Impulsively hostile, explosive, or subject to paranoid rage.
- Hyperaggressive and easily agitated, with poor self-control and limited capacity for socialization.
- Poorly socialized and insensitive to others.
- Having rigid tendencies, and subject to over-controlled hostility that may be expressed in unexpected assaults.

When psychologists explore the background history of individuals exhibiting these characteristics, they find that they may also have had a history of committing aggressive acts, had problems in other jobs, and been abused or lived in abusive environments.

Preemployment screening concerns are strengthened when verified by past behavior of candidates. Further support for these concerns comes from retrospective analyses of the characteristics of police who have abused force. Moreover, these concerns contrast to how police, as a group, are described on psychological tests. The literature shows that police generally score well within normal limits on personality measures (For a complete review, see Lowman, 1989).

Factors that dictate screening practices. Police preemployment screening is designed to prevent the occurrence of several kinds of problem police behavior, only one of which is the use of excessive force. Consequently, screening has become psychopathology-driven, that is, focused on identifying the characteristics of bad officers. Less is known about the characteristics of good officers, or about how career experiences buffer personal tendencies. Although clinical information is critical to employment decisions for highly sensitive jobs, this psychopathology focus has influenced the screening process. It has shaped screening methodology, in particular the types of instruments that are used most frequently, and it has fostered a "screening out" model that makes innovation, as well as validation, more difficult.

These issues were apparent in the interview responses. Psychologists said they made limited use

---

1. Scales 4, 6, 8, and 9 were of particular concern to most of the psychologists.

of risk assessment models, situational testing, or job simulations, even though these models could incorporate a wider range of information for making decisions. Moreover, they could also provide a way to judge the validity of the narrow combinations of scale elevations on paper-pencil tests and self-report data. While developing such models requires an initial commitment of police department resources, it is likely that departments who use psychologists have an extensive data base that could be helpful in this development.

Screening practices must satisfy several other requirements:

■ Ensuring that screening predictors are linked to job performance criteria.

▣ Ensuring against discrimination by conforming to fair employment practices, affirmative action plans, and civil rights laws.

■ Developing procedures that protect sensitive information.

These significant tasks are necessary to maintain the integrity and fairness of the screening process and to ensure that psychological tests are used in a manner consistent with ethical standards.

In the context of a psychopathology-driven screening approach, it is not surprising that psychologists have relied on a fairly traditional battery of tests having some research support. This is a particularly sensitive issue when it comes to tests such as the MMPI–MMPI-2.

Although the MMPI is apparently the mainstay of the current police screening process, it was never developed to be used in this manner. Unable to be applied in competitive Federal employee selection, yet mandated for use by the California Peace Officer Standards and Training (POST) Commission and agencies in a number of other States, the MMPI remains a subject of controversy and legal debate. It is one of the most widely used personality tests and continues to be used for the evaluation of job candidates (Matarazzo, 1990).[2]

Issues in predicting behavior. Issues relative to screening candidates for propensity to violence are particularly relevant to the debate on the merits of routinely testing incumbent officers. The use of psychological assessments in this manner assumes that psychologists can reliably predict behavior. There is no strong body of evidence that supports this assumption. Although significant strides have been made, psychologists are generally respectful of how the complexity of human behavior, and all its contingencies, limits the accuracy of scientific prediction. This caution was reflected in this study by the fact that psychologists were able to describe profiles from clinical data but were less conclusive on how well pre-employment screening data successfully predicted violence on the job. Although followup data are collected by most of the psychologists, for the most part the results remain inconclusive with respect to the use of excessive force. For all of these reasons, psychologists' efforts have been directed to predicting patrol behavior in relation to broad standards of police effectiveness rather than to a use-of-force criterion.

New directions in screening. The findings of this study show that preemployment screening is ripe for much-needed innovation. Opportunities for developing new screening technology that may be more responsive to predicting violence are occurring for reasons that have nothing to do with excessive force. In particular, forthcoming developments related to the American With Disabilities Act will change current screening processes by differentiating test use on the basis of different criteria for pre- and post-job-offer testing. Since the specific criteria have yet to be published by the Equal Employment Opportunity Commission, the future direction of psychological screening cannot be predicted. All the evidence, however, suggests that the MMPI, and tests of that nature, will be administered postoffer and used as clinical appraisals (Crosby, 1979) to assess the presence of psychopathology and its potential to interfere with a police officer's functions.

---

2. It is too soon to know how a recently settled court case (Soroka v. Dayton Hudson) will affect the use of personality inventories like the MMPI in employee selection for sensitive positions.

Preoffer testing is likely to undergo substantial change. New screening technologies and high-performance analytic methods will emerge that consider the following:

■ How police candidates make decisions.

■ How they process information under stressful conditions.

■ How they solve problems consistent with community policing.

■ How they interact with people.

■ How they control situations.

Automated assessment systems, interactive video testing, assessment centers, job simulations, and role playing exercises all hold promise to meet these goals. Before new instrumentation can be used, however, there must be support for the extensive research needed to develop a job-related data base to show how well new assessment techniques can predict performance. Moreover, continued evaluation will be required so that a longitudinal validation of the testing process can take place.

Finally, related to discussions of the status of screening police candidates are the concerns that emerged in the previously described clinical profiles that implicated other factors in excessive force (such as previous job-related experiences, early-stage career problems, and patrol style). The screening findings in this study suggest that current assessment methods do not always detect such factors; thus police departments should be cautious in using current screening techniques alone to prevent excessive-force problems.

Findings on Testing Incumbent Officers

Psychologists were sharply divided on using psychological tests to routinely evaluate incumbent officers. Those opposed recommended alternatives to this practice; overall study findings provided strong support for using other methods to periodically evaluate incumbents.

Psychologists were asked their opinion on testing incumbent officers to detect violence proneness.

■ 43 percent said they favored testing.

■ 43 percent said they opposed testing.

■ 12 percent said "it depends."

■ 2 percent said they did not know.

The sample is sharply divided on this issue. With the exception of those who said "it depends," citing their experience in testing officers for special unit assignments, exactly the same number of psychologists favored and opposed this practice. Of those in favor, 56 percent would use the tests that are currently used in preemployment screening. Only a small number indicated a preference for greater emphasis on clinical interviews or performance-based testing. Since all police psychologists responded to this question, including those who did not do screening, it is possible that some of the psychologists were unfamiliar with technical issues related to the psychological assessment of tenured employees.

Psychologists opposed to this practice expressed concerns. They questioned:

■ The logistics and practical problems involved with large scale testing.

■ The lack of normative test data and related false positive identifications.

■ Privacy problems inherent to department treatment of the information.

■ Threats of litigation.

■ Fairness issues.

As alternatives to testing, they recommended the use of:

■ Behavioral early warning systems.

■ Remedial training for officers.

■ Corrective counseling programs focused on changing excessive-force behavior.

■ Supervisor training to recognize precursors of excessive-force problems.

- Peer review.

This last alternative, peer review, was least endorsed.

Concerns about the logistics of implementing wide-scale testing on a routine basis should be considered in light of the previously reported finding that there is a lack of coordination of psychological services in police departments.

At best, findings on this important question appear to be inconclusive if one considers only the specific findings reported above. However, when the full sample of psychologists stated their opinions on how best to reduce excessive force in police departments, psychological testing did not have the highest priority.

Identification and Remediation of Excessive Force

To identify individual officers prone to excessive force, psychologists recommended increasing the behavioral monitoring function. To accomplish an overall reduction of excessive force in a police department, improved training was recommended.

When asked to select the best method of identifying officers prone to excessive force, psychologists chose the following:

- Monitoring, cited by 46 percent.
- Psychological screening, cited by 23 percent.
- Administrative review, cited by 14 percent.
- Training, cited by 12 percent.
- Counseling, cited by 5 percent.

When asked to recommend ways departments can help reduce use of excessive force, psychologists cited the following:

- Training was cited by 62 percent.
- Counseling was cited by 40 percent.
- Monitoring was cited by 38 percent.
- Screening was cited by 32 percent.
- Organizational interventions were cited by 25 percent.
- Research was cited by 15 percent.
- Fitness-for-duty evaluations were cited by 12 percent.

Even though 28 psychologists agreed with the recommendation to test incumbent officers periodically, the findings above do not fully support that recommendation. More psychologists recommended monitoring (46 percent) than testing (23 percent) to identify officers prone to excessive force. When asked which functions of the police psychologist should be increased to reduce the incidence of police use of excessive force, they recommended training and, to a lesser extent, counseling as the more viable interventions, in contrast to evaluation. In fact, fitness evaluations, which would be more consistent with evaluating incumbents, constituted the least recommended intervention to reduce excessive force.

The finding that ascribes a lower priority for the value of research in resolving excessive-force problems is of concern since widely accepted interventions generally have limited empirical support. Police psychology is essentially practice driven, often at the expense of evaluation. Consistent evaluation, however, would strengthen the use of all intervention functions, determine what works and what does not, and could provide new information on more effective ways to intervene in excessive force. Thus, the research function presents an opportunity to affect the behavior of the total organization.

Part 5. Discussion of Findings

This research brings a new level of understanding to how police officers cross the line to abuse force. It initiates the development of an etiology of excessive force, a necessary forerunner to exploring effective ways of managing this pressing police problem. Although the findings address only the most serious of offenders—officers who are referred to psychologists for serious infractions of department policies on use of force—this is a population that researchers and policymakers need to know more about.

The findings suggest that conventional wisdom characterizing serious offenders as only a "few bad apples" does not appear to describe most officers who become involved in excessive force. Rather, excessive force is enacted within a broader context. Different types of personal and job-related situations place different types of officers at risk for excessive force complaints. In this regard, use of excessive force is decidedly more complex and multidimensional than the "few bad apples" theory would imply. Officer personality features represent only one element of the problem. In some instances, personality and situational factors interact, but in others organizational practices are more strongly implicated.

Police psychologists appear to be in a good position to help police departments deal with excessive force matters, given their existing active presence in these agencies. In some respects, the detailing of the extent of police psychology practice and the various functions performed in police departments constitutes a major finding of this study. To date, this information has not been well-documented for police managers.

It could be argued that police managers have accepted police psychologists as part of a strategy to manage the key elements of the organization—its human resources. However, there is little evidence to suggest that police departments have adopted a human resource development approach to managing personnel issues. Moreover, police departments place little emphasis on tapping psychologists' understanding of what causes aggression and violence and of the principles of behavior change.

For police psychology to be fully effective in police departments, particularly for excessive force concerns, there needs to be a greater emphasis on prevention and on involving the police psychologist in a proactive approach to managing human resources. Providing interventions that consider officer career needs as well as the demands on the organization over time is preferable to reacting to officers and the command structure only when there is trouble.

Within this context, the prevalence of excessive force needs to be considered as symptomatic of a systemwide problem that implicates administrative policies as well as key elements of the human resource system, that is, selection, training, and supervision. Psychologists are involved in different ways with all these elements, but a coherent structure that integrates services and maximizes impact on both the individual officers and the organization seems to be lacking. A more effective structure would also help to clarify the distinctions between predicting and managing excessive force in order to address all elements of unwarranted force.

Predicting and Managing Excessive Force

Establishing a balance between predicting and managing excessive force is important to reducing the occurrence of these incidents. Prediction was strongly emphasized by the Christopher Commission and the Kolt Report in their focus on psychological testing (see page 4). However, those recommendations make the assumption that psychologists will be given the resources to conduct the rigorous research that is necessary to strengthen predictive accuracy of psychological testing beyond its current rudimentary level. Since the commitment of time and money for important test validation research has not materialized in the past, it may be unrealistic to assume that departments will now be able to devote scarce resources to more extensive validation efforts. Consequently, police policymakers could be faced with the choice of either reliably predicting use of excessive force for a limited number of officers or managing use of excessive force for all officers. The more balanced approach encourages attending to the front end of the system (selection) while building in safeguards throughout (monitoring, training, supervision).

To achieve this balance, existing departmental resources need to be systematically integrated to provide a comprehensive response to excessive force. Simply using a new screening test or trying a new training program will not achieve balance and will address the problem in a piecemeal fashion. Rather, there needs to be a coherent framework that incorporates the department's psychological services into a concerted effort to curb abusive police practices, like the one discussed on page 1.

While research findings describe what psychologists can offer to a police agency, departments do not appear to have used psychologists as a constant resource. Rather, they seem to use them on an "as needed" basis and as protection against liability from charges of negligence. The range of organizational safeguards that can be applied by psychological services has thus not been fully exploited. Police administrators should rethink how they are using psychologists. Clearly, screening out potential violators, counseling problem officers, and evaluating them for fitness to perform the police function are critical activities. However, there is a strong need for ongoing prevention activities that lead to early identification of, and intervention in, police problems. It is here where psychologists can have a strong impact, but these activities are pursued with less diligence than the other ones.

Hidden Statistics and Policy-Relevant Information

The rich descriptive data that shaped the profiles of officers at risk for excessive force demonstrate that psychologists collect what could be called the "hidden statistic"—human resource information that is relevant to policy. These profiles offer many benefits:

■ They initiate an etiology of excessive force.

■ They provide insight into the complexity of the phenomenon.

■ They highlight the need for a range of systemic interventions.

■ They address the excessive-force problem both from the individual officer and the organizational practice perspectives.

■ They underscore how behavior can be reinforced or sanctioned by tradition-clad mores and values.

These descriptive data support the notion that excessive force is a systemwide problem and in some instances may reflect a dysfunctional system. A related and important issue is the extent to which system interventions are limited by the status of police psychology practices as well as the lack of coordination of these services in police departments.

Status of Police Psychology Practice

Significant questions directly related to the scope and direction of police psychology practice have been raised in this study. The fact that fewer psychologists are involved in the monitoring function may be related to the finding that two-thirds of the research sample are consultants and provide services to an average of 10 departments. One might question if these conditions tend to fragment the practice of police psychology. Except for psychologists who designated evaluation as a specialty with no involvement in other forms of service delivery, and for some on command staffs, the majority of the psychologists surveyed appear to do screening for one department, counseling for another, and training for still another.

The shortage of psychologists who are experienced with police populations may be one reason for this practice, thereby encouraging psychologists to structure their business to handle several contracts simultaneously. The profit motive of these arrangements is another, and the failure of police departments to use psychologists as part of a human resource development model is still another. Nevertheless, fragmented services can contribute to the lack of coordination and credibility of services within police departments. They can impede effective delivery of psychological services, and they can seriously hinder the continued growth of police psychological services.

Fragmentation of services is the parent to stagnation and obsolescence. Fragmentation precludes psychologists from fully learning the police culture, from seeing their work within the context of the overall system, and from empirically evaluating their work. From the standpoint of human resource development, fragmentation keeps in place a clinical-crisis orientation that focuses on individuals at the expense of organizational development. Finally, it may not even be cost-beneficial.

The findings particularly underscore the lack of a coherent strategy to systematically integrate the functions performed by psychologists that are relevant to the management of excessive force and the limited use of human resource strategies in police departments. Whether the lack of coherent

frameworks is driven by police department traditions that keep psychologists at arm's length or by the current status of police psychology practice is not clear from this study. It is an area that needs to be clarified since it may be central to important concerns raised by the Christopher Commission and the Kolt Report relative to police psychology and excessive force.

This study has shown that psychologists not only contribute specific technical assistance through the core functions of their profession but also offer substantial resources to police organizations, as evidenced by the wealth of information in the clinical description of excessive force. When used to full advantage, psychologists can provide departments with information about organizational problems and potential interventions.

The next phase of this research will be to explore these issues in greater detail through indepth examinations of model programs in police departments that used their psychologists to develop interventions to respond to excessive force. The many issues that emerged in this phase of the study will be further examined in selected departments, and questions for future policy-related research will be determined.

Appendix:

Literature Review
and Implications for
Excessive Force

The literature on use of nonlethal excessive force remains relatively sparse. However, there are some areas of research that are pertinent to this study. Clearly, excessive force cannot be discussed without addressing deadly force. Most of what is known about force pertains to police shootings and killings in contrast to use of nonlethal force. Other lines of relevant research include predicting violence, particularly through the use of psychological tests, and managing the use of force through training and organizational interventions.

Use of Lethal Force

The literature shows a 20-year emphasis on reducing police use of deadly force (Blumberg, 1989). One of the most important and consistent findings of this research is that restrictive firearm policies have been instrumental in reducing police shootings of citizens (Geller and Karalis, 1981; Sherman, 1983; Geller and Scott, 1992). Until recently, policy-related research on use of nondeadly force has not received equal attention.

For the most part, police psychologists, too, focused primarily on the use of deadly force. This emphasis is reflected in the practice of providing psychological support to officers involved in departmental shootings and in on-duty traumatic incidents. The development and implementation of a short-term crisis response for affected officers, the Critical Incident Debriefing Response (see Reese, Horn, and Dunning, 1990, for a comprehensive review) is used on a fairly regular basis by police departments (Zelig, 1986).

Research on the critical-incident response is scant and generally methodologically flawed. However, findings are relatively consistent in documenting the reactions of officers during and after these incidents. Essentially, the findings support anecdotal evidence suggesting that many police officers experience psychological reactions in varying degrees that include a wide range of perceptual distortions that occur during the shooting, and a period of emotional disruption following the incident. Reactions can be manifested in somatic conditions such as sleep disturbances and in varied

emotional and cognitive symptoms of distress (Solomon and Horn, 1986; Bohl, 1991; Nielsen, 1991). There appears to be some consensus that these reactions are due to involvement in violence in contrast to being responses of violent officers. Currently, there are few data to support the contention that officers involved in police shootings are violence prone. Rather, they are described as generally troubled by the incident and fearful for their careers. The consistency of these responses drives police departments to provide an immediate and psychologically supportive response to officers involved in deadly force incidents.

Use of nondeadly force elicits a decidedly different response in police departments. In these instances, officers charged with excessive force may be referred to a psychologist only after cumulative incidents and often through department disciplinary proceedings. However, rather than being referred for clinical support, the officers may need to have "fitness-for-duty" evaluations to determine if they are psychologically able to carry weapons and function as police officers (Ostrov, 1993). It has been suggested that fitness-for-duty referrals are perceived as punitive, represent career threats, and elicit officer resistance to intervention efforts. One asks, do these referrals represent the best conditions for changing behavior and preventing excessive force? In many cases, fitness-for-duty referrals may be appropriate. However, when used as the standard department response to police use of excessive force, rather than as only one alternative, they may limit the effectiveness of psychologists to prevent further abuse of force.

Shift in Emphasis to Nonlethal Force

The trend for psychologists, criminal justice researchers, and practitioners to address police shootings and killings with comparatively more vigor than they address the use of nonlethal violence appears to be changing. The topic of police violence was the focus of a special edition of *Annals of the American Academy of Political and Social Science* (1980). Generally, this collection of essays approached physical and nonlethal violence from a theoretical perspective, an important threshold to cross to define essential determinants of police nonlethal violence and effective ways to manage it.

This shift in emphasis away from the deadly force preoccupation is also reflected in a growing number of research studies that examine elements of nondeadly force within a broader context instead of documenting frequency of occurrence. One of the earliest observational studies in this area (Reiss, 1968) concluded that use of force occurred infrequently. The more recent findings of Bayley and Garafalo (1989) support Reiss. They observed officer tactics that either reduced or increased use of violence and argued that use of force, including verbal aggression, occurred less often than might be expected. Their study elaborated on the context of excessive force and identified three decision points in violent encounters—the initial contact, the processing, and the exit stages.

Other studies that examine police behavior from a broader perspective include Worden's examination of the influences of attitudinal and situational factors (1990), and two projects that treat excessive force as a dynamic process and use field research to shape training that addresses contextual aspects of excessive force (Fyfe, 1989; Nicoletti, 1990). While a variety of use-of-force training programs are beginning to appear in the literature (for a comprehensive review see Geller and Scott, 1992), the Fyfe and the Nicoletti projects are noteworthy because their efforts provide a data-based foundation for training programs on excessive force.

Research-Driven Training: A Context for Excessive Force

Fyfe (1989) questioned why police departments treat successful resolutions of violent police-citizen confrontations as the result of a "mystical sixth sense" and concluded that the absence of relevant data to support skill-based training may account for this perception. His report on the Metro Dade Police Violence Reduction Project shows how contextual data provided a foundation for

violence reduction training designed to reduce use of excessive force. This project developed content for an intensive 3-day role play training based on direct observations of more than 1,000 police-citizen confrontations and the types of violent encounters occurring most frequently. Training was provided for half of the observed officers, with the others serving as a control group. Followup data showed that the training had positive effects on how potentially violent situations were approached and resolved by officers. These data also revealed that some officers were unable to resolve these situations because they were not assertive. Torres (1992) subsequently reported that this type of training was accompanied by a decrease in reported incidents of citizen dissatisfaction despite an increase in calls for service.

Nicoletti (1990) reported on a threat-assessment and deescalation-of-force training program for police recruits. It was subsequently expanded as an inservice program for all officers in the Denver Police Department (Nicoletti, 1993). Training needs were identified in survey data showing that officer overreactions and use of force were related to inadequate training in situation control, which elevated officer stress level and degraded confidence. Using psychological theories as a foundation for training content, the program addressed the perceptual frameworks and influence of arousal levels on information processing when officers were exposed to simulated violence. His findings bear some similarity to Fyfe's observations that use of force results from the officer's lack of skills and the unintentional provocation caused by the time constraints of the "split second syndrome." The observations strike a needed balance in addressing influences brought by the officer and by the organization. This balance was alluded to by Toch (1969; 1992) who contended that violence in police officers is not always a function of personality but may also be due to organizational influences.

These field studies are more consistent with the conceptual framework advanced by Binder and Scharf (1980). They viewed physical force as a result of a sequence of transactions and decisions rather than as a unitary phenomenon. They argued that excessive force situations develop in phases; they do not happen in a split second. Their view was supported, in part, by the report to the Governor of the New York State Commission on Criminal Justice and the Use of Force (1987), which suggested that complex situational factors influence an officer's decision o use force.

The above lines of research begin to provide a fuller and more realistic context for understanding excessive force and differ from incident-driven statistical models that report only the frequency of complaints. They question stereotypes about use of excessive force occurring in a split second and view it as one outcome of a complex decision-making process that is influenced by multiple variables interacting to either escalate or defuse the process. These approaches remove the "inevitable" from beliefs about excessive force and are compatible with cognitive-psychological theories of aggression (Eron, 1987; Berkowitz, 1990). According to these theorists, aggression is a learned behavior. As such, it can be unlearned. Moreover, contextual studies provide better support for training to build competency-based skills and tactics to broaden officers' repertoire of strategies to use in confrontations. In this regard, they support the training emphasis on officer safety by supplementing physical proficiency training with non-physical tactics.

Psychological Screening of Police Recruits

Data-driven training innovations present one promising approach to reducing excessive force. It is less certain whether preemployment evaluation of police candidates holds similar promise. The research on screening has emphasized the prediction of effective work performance. Prediction of isolated, low-base-rate, or infrequently occurring behaviors such as future violence has been limited because of concerns about false positive identifications.

Inwald reports that prediction equations derived from the Inwald Personality Inventory have been successful in predicting poor work performance marked by excessive absences, disciplinary interviews, and job terminations. While job terminations may be due to excessive force, Inwald does not make these claims (Shusman, Inwald, and Knatz, 1987).

Hargrave and Berner (1984), in one of the most comprehensive research studies on police psychological screening, identified the need for officers to control aggression as one psychological attribute necessary for police performance. Hargrave, Hiatt, and Gaffney (1988) subsequently identified an index of psychological test scales that increased accuracy in predicting highly aggressive behavior in police applicants and in officers who became physically assaultive. Generally, however, the literature relating test indices to excessive force remains sparse, and it is not clear whether police psychologists specifically test for behavioral propensities to engage in violence when determining suitability for a police career.

A more fundamental question is the emphasis that police agencies place on the psychological screening function. Police personnel policy may have expectations for preemployment screening that are inconsistent with what it can realistically accomplish. In this regard, it has not been established if assessments are expected to provide a type of mental health snapshot of an individual's current status or, on the other hand, to provide a mental health seal of approval that is good for the individual's entire career. The latter represents an ambitious and unrealistic goal for any evaluation method because it suggests that candidates at age 21 will be the same at age 41, leaving no room for personal changes resulting from experience, growth and maturity, or the powerful influence of the police culture. If viewed from the former, more narrow perspective of providing a mental health snapshot of an individual's present status, it may be that current preemployment evaluations are doing what they are methodologically capable of doing—identifying psychopathology in police applicants who are emotionally unfit.

Prediction of Police Violence and Risk Assessment

Another side of the argument questions if assessment techniques, in contrast to discrete tests, have been fully exploited to improve the predictive power of low-base-rate behaviors such as police violence. Monahan (1981), who found very little empirical support for the accuracy of clinical predictions of dangerousness in the mentally ill, also discussed the limitations of that relatively sparse body of research. His review of the literature is frequently cited as conclusive evidence that mental health professionals are unable to predict dangerous behavior, leading him to comment on how quickly and uncritically his findings were accepted (Monahan, 1988). Whether predictions of police officer violence should be compared to predictions about mentally disordered individuals in civil commitment proceedings is debatable, but Monahan's cautions are generally raised when prediction of police violence is questioned.

More recently, Monahan (1992) modified his views and described a series of exploratory studies by the MacArthur Foundation Research Network on Mental Health and the Law. These studies are investigating actuarially based risk assessment models to determine if they can improve the accuracy of predictions. The risk assessment model looks at risk "markers" across multiple domains, including environment/situational, dispositional, historical, and clinical (Monahan and Steadman, in press). According to Otto (1992), advances in prediction techniques that come from "second generation" prediction research may hold promise for decreasing error rates in predictions of dangerousness by mental health professionals. They may also hold promise for preemployment screening of police recruits. Currently, it is unknown if these models can be adapted to assessing police officer violence, but Trompetter (1993) and Ostrov (1993) discuss methods that can be explored to help identify individuals who may be at risk for the possibility of police abuse of force.

Trompetter culled the professional literature and identified 29 variables that have been shown to correlate with adult violent behavior and called for a stronger emphasis in police preemployment assessment on the historical antecedents that signify recurrent violence. He urged that police preemployment screening interviews and psychological tests be more sharply focused on identifying these variables as "red flags" that require a more focused investigation into a candidate's predisposition to engage in unnecessary or excessive force. Ostrov discussed an "expert systems model" that develops a "trend line" across behavioral domains. Based on the theory that violence is never an isolated act, he looks for trends that signify an individual's socialization into accepting violence and escalation of violence over time, as well as personal tendencies that contraindicate expression of violence.

The work of Trompetter and Ostrov, along with that of Monahan, lay the groundwork for exploring risk assessment models that provide a more comprehensive framework for behavior predictions. By including varied domains, researchers can sample a larger universe of behavior and can evaluate a broader span of information. Hence, while engaging in a violent act may be a low-base-rate behavior, the precursor behaviors, or "risk markers" that signify a history of aggression across situations may occur with greater frequency across domains and strengthen predictions. These models provide a contrast to current paradigms that have been modestly successful in linking narrow psychological test variables to a broad spectrum of police behavior. Whether they provide analogs for police selection and satisfy requirements for high predictive validity is unknown, but they do merit systematic evaluation in any effort to enlarge the scope and reliability of current preemployment screening. Pending careful evaluation, they may provide a needed adjunct to current screening methods.

References

Ash, P., Slora, K.B., and Britton, C.F. (1990). "Police Agency Officer Selection Practices," *Journal of Police Science and Administration*, 17:258–269.

Bayley, D., and Garafalo, J. (1989). "The Management of Violence by Police Patrol Officers," *Criminology*, 27:1–27.

Berkowitz, L. (1990). "On the Formation and Regulation of Anger and Aggression: A Cognitive Neoassocianistic Analysis," *American Psychologist*, 45:494–503.

Binder, A., and Scharf, D. (1980). "The Violent Police-Citizen Encounter," *Annals of the American Academy of Political and Social Science*, 452:111–121.

Blumberg, M. (1989). "Controlling Police Use of Deadly Force: Assessing Two Decades of Progress." In R.G. Dunham and G.P. Alpert (eds.), *Critical Issues in Policing: Contemporary Readings*. Prospect Heights, Illinois: Waveland Press.

Bohl, N.K. (1991). "The Effectiveness of Brief Psychological Interventions in Police Officers After Critical Incidents." In J.T. Reese, J.M. Horn, and C. Dunning (eds.), *Critical Incidents in Policing, Revised*. Washington, D.C.: U.S. Government Printing Office.

Burbeck, E., and Furnham, A. (1985). "Police Officer Selection: A Critical Review of the Literature," *Journal of Police Science and Administration*, 13:58–69.

Crosby, A. (1979). "The Psychological Examination in Police Selection," *Journal of Police Science and Administration*, 7:215–229.

Delprino, R.P., and Bahn, C. (1988). "National Survey of the Extent and Nature of Psychological Services in Police Departments," *Professional Psychology: Research and Practice*, 19(4):421–425.

Eron, L.D. (1987). "The Development of Aggressive Behavior From the Perspective of a Developing Behaviorism," *American Psychologist*, 42(5): 435–442.

Fyfe, J.J. (1989). "Police/Citizen Violence Reduction Project," *FBI Law Enforcement Bulletin*, 58 (May):18–23.

Geller, W.A., and Karalis, K.J. (1981). *Split-Second Decision: Shooting Of and By Chicago Police*. Chicago: Chicago Law Enforcement Study Group.

Geller, W., and Scott, M.S. (1992). *Deadly Force: What We Know*. Washington, D.C.: Police Executive Research Forum.

Hargrave, G.E., and Berner, J.G. (1984). *POST Psychological Screening Manual*. Sacramento: California Commission on Peace Officer Standards and Training.

Hargrave, G.E., Hiatt, D., and Gaffney, T.W. (1988). "F+4+9+Cn: An MMPI Measure of Aggression in Law Enforcement Officers and Applicants," *Journal of Police Science and Administration*, 16(4):268–273.

Independent Commission To Study the Los Angeles Police Department (1991). *Report of the Independent Commission on the Los Angeles Police Department*. (Los Angeles: Author).

Kerner Commission (1968). *National Advisory Commission on Civil Disorder Report*. New York: E.P. Dutton.

Kirschman, E., Scrivner, E., Ellison, K., and Marcy, C. (1992). "Work and Well Being: Lessons From Law Enforcement." In J.C. Quick, L.R. Murphy, and J.J. Hurrell (eds.), *Stress and Well Being at Work: Assessments and Interventions for Occupational Mental Health*. Washington, D.C.: American Psychological Association.

Kolt, J.G. et al. (1992). *Los Angeles County Sheriff's Department: A Report by James G. Kolt and Staff*. (Los Angeles: Author).

Lowman, R.L. (1989). *Pre-employment Screening for Psychopathology: A Guide to Professional Practice*. Florida: Professional Resource Exchange.

Mattarazzo, J.D. (1990). "Psychological Assessment Versus Psychological Testing: Validation From Binet to the School, Clinic and Courtroom," *American Psychologist*, 45:999–1017.

Monahan, J. (1981). *The Clinical Prediction of Violent Behavior*. Washington, D.C.: U.S. Government Printing Office.

Monahan, J. (1988). "Risk Assessment of Violence Among the Mentally Disordered: Generating Useful Knowledge," *International Journal of Law and Psychiatry*, 11:249–257.

Monahan, J. (1992). "Mental Disorder and Violent Behavior: Perceptions and Evidence," *American Psychologist*, 47(4): 511–521.

Monahan, J., and Steadman, H.J. (eds.) (in press). "Toward a Rejuvenation of Risk Assessment Research." In *Violence and Mental Disorder: Developments in Risk Assessment*. Chicago: University of Chicago Press.

Moore, M.H., and Stephens, D.W. (1991). *Beyond Command and Control: The Strategic Management of Police Departments*. Washington, D.C.: Police Executive Research Forum.

Murphy, J. (1972). "Current Practices in the Use of Psychological Testing by Police Agencies," *Journal of Criminal Law, Criminology and Police Science*, 63:570–576.

New York State Commission on Criminal Justice and the Use of Force (1987). *Report to the Governor*, 3 vols. New York.

Nicoletti, J. (1990). "Training for De-escalation of Force," *The Police Chief*, July:37–39.

Nicoletti, J. (1993). "Training for De-escalation of Force," paper presented at the Annual Convention of the American Psychological Association, August, Toronto, Canada.

Nielsen, E. (1991). "Factors Influencing the Nature of Posttraumatic Stress Disorders." In J.T. Reese, J.M. Horn, and C. Dunning (eds.), *Critical Incidents in Policing, Revised.* Washington, D.C.: U.S. Government Printing Office.

Ostrov, E. (1993). "Prediction of Police Officer Violence," paper presented at the Annual Convention of the American Psychological Association, August, Toronto, Canada.

Otto, R. (1992). "The Prediction of Dangerous Behavior: A Review and Analysis of 'Second Generation' Research," *Forensic Reports*, 5:103–133.

Parisher, D., Rios, B., and Riley, R. (1979). "Psychologists and Psychological Services in Urban Police Departments," *Professional Psychology*, 10:6–7.

Reese, J.T. (1987). *A History of Police Psychological Services.* Washington, D.C.: U.S. Department of Justice.

Reese, J.T., Horn, J.M., and Dunning, C. (1990). *Critical Incident in Policing.* Washington, D.C.: U.S. Government Printing Office.

Reiser, M. (1972). *The Police Department Psychologist.* Springfield, Illinois: Charles C. Thomas.

Reiss, A.J. (1968). "Police Brutality—Answers to Key Questions," *Transaction*, 5:10–19.

Reiss, A.J. (1980). "Controlling Police Use of Deadly Force," *Annals of the American Academy of Political and Social Science*, 452 (November):122–134.

Scrivner, E. (1988). "Organizational Interventions in Law Enforcement," paper presented at the Annual Convention of the American Psychological Association, August, Atlanta, Georgia.

Scrivner, E. (1992). "Police Psychology: A Resource for Contemporary Police Managers," paper presented at the Annual Convention of the American Psychological Association, August, Washington, D.C.

Sherman, L. (1983). "Reducing Police Gun Use: Critical Events, Administrative Policy, and Organizational Change." In Maurice Punch (ed.), *Control in the Police Organization.* Cambridge, Massachusetts: MIT Press.

Shusman, E.J., Inwald, R.E., and Knatz, H.F. (1987). "A Cross Validation Study of Police Recruit Performance as Predicted by the IPI and MMPI," *Journal of Police Science and Administration*, 15:162–169.

Solomon, R.M., and Horn, J.M. (1986). "Post-Shooting Traumatic Reactions: A Pilot Study." In J.T. Reese and H.A. Goldstein (eds.), *Psychological Services for Law Enforcement.* Washington, D.C.: U.S. Government Printing Office.

Stratton, J.G. (1980). "Psychological Services for Police," *Journal of Police Science and Administration*, 8:31–39.

Toch, H. (1969). *Violent Men: An Inquiry Into the Psychology of Violence.* Revised edition (1992). Washington, D.C.: American Psychological Association.

Torres, J.A. (1992). "Making Sensitivity Training Work," *Police Chief*, August:32–33.

Trompetter, P.S. (1993). "Pre-employment Psychological Screening of Violence-Prone Peace Officer Applicants," *The Journal of California Law Enforcement*, 27(1):16–19.

U.S. Department of Justice, Federal Bureau of Investigation (1984). *State and Local Law Enforcement Training Needs in the United States.* Washington, D.C.: U.S. Government Printing Office.

U.S. Department of Justice, Federal Bureau of Investigation (1990). *Uniform Crime Reports for the United States.* Washington, D.C.: U.S. Government Printing Office.

Wilson, J.Q., and Kelling, G.L. (1982). "Police and Neighborhood Safety: Broken Windows," *Atlantic Monthly*, March:29–38.

Worden, R.E. (1990). "Situational and Attitudinal Explanations of Police Behavior: A Theoretical Reappraisal and Empirical Assessment," *Law and Society Review*, 23(4):667–711.

Zelig, M. (1986). "Research Needs in the Study of Post Shooting Trauma." In J.T. Reese and H.A. Goldstein (eds.), *Psychological Services for Law Enforcement.* Washington, D.C.: U.S. Government Printing Office.